I HAVE A LEARNING DISABILITY, AND IT'S OKAY!

Written by
Dr. William M. Bauer

Illustrated by
Mallory Hill

WestBow Press books may be ordered through booksellers or by contacting:

WestBow Press
A Division of Thomas Nelson & Zondervan
1663 Liberty Drive
Bloomington, IN 47403
www.westbowpress.com
844-714-3454

Interior Image Credit: Mallory Hill

ISBN: 978-1-6642-4336-1 (sc)
ISBN: 978-1-6642-4337-8 (e)

Library of Congress Control Number: 2021912589

Print information available on the last page.

WestBow Press rev. date: 09/13/2021

WESTBOW
PRESS®
A DIVISION OF THOMAS NELSON
& ZONDERVAN

I HAVE A LEARNING DISABILITY, AND
IT'S OKAY!

About the Author:

Dr. William M. (Bill) Bauer is a licensed clinical counselor in the rural Mid-Ohio Valley area who was a former classroom teacher, principal, and college professor. He has worked with children and adults with disabilities all of his life and hopes that this book brings an understanding to children with disabilities, their teachers, and their classmates. Dr. Bauer was born with a severe hearing impairment.

THIS BOOK IS DEDICATED TO:

ALL PEOPLE WITH DISABILITIES WHOSE LIVES ARE SHARED IN THIS BOOK SERIES TO MAKE THE WORLD A BETTER PLACE. ALL WE WANT IS TO BE ACCEPTED AS WE ARE, HAVE FRIENDS, LIVE IN OUR COMMUNITIES AND TO DREAM AS OUR NON-DISABLED PEERS.

SPECIAL THANKS TO MY WIFE, MARY ELLA, DAUGHTER MADISON RYSER, HER HUSBAND ANDREW AND GRANDSON JACK.

#GRANTSPEED. LOVE YOU, SON

To:

From:

Forewords:

I have had the pleasure of working with Dr. Bauer in the professional education and mental health fields for over two decades, and this book series is his latest outstanding work to help young people understand and accept differences. Each title focuses on a uniqueness and assures us that "it is OKAY!"

Dr. Stephanie Starcher
Public School Superintendent

Being different is OK! Every effort to erase stigma surrounding our differences is important. The earlier we start, the better chance we have at preventing stigma from even occurring. I had the honor of meeting Dr. Bill Bauer when I was in college, and it is no surprise his work as a mental health advocate would transpire into this series of books. I'm thankful for his commitment to celebrating our differences.

Nick Gehlfuss, MFA, Actor, film and television.
Currently, Dr. Halstead, Chicago Med.

This book series by Dr. William Bauer — my good friend Bill — fills a niche in children's literature that embraces diversity and self esteem. This series is not only important, but extremely fun. As founder of Orphans International, I look forward to reading these stories to children of all faiths and abilities around the world. This book is indeed a living testament to Bill's own son. The world is a better place because of Bill Bauer! #GrantSpeed

James Jay Dudley Luce, Founder Orphans International Worldwide,
International Entrepreneur

HI!
MY NAME IS SAM, AND I HAVE A LEARNING DISABILITY.

I DON'T LEARN THE WAY EVERYONE IN MY CLASS DOES. IT DOESN'T MEAN I AM DUMB. I JUST LEARN DIFFERENTLY. NOT EVERYONE LEARNS THE SAME WAY.

I HAVE TROUBLE READING. SOME PEOPLE HAVE TROUBLE WITH MATH OR WRITING.

SOMETIMES I GET MY LETTERS MIXED UP, SOMETIMES I HAVE TROUBLE SAYING WORDS. SOMETIMES I CANNOT REMEMBER WHAT I JUST READ IN A BOOK A MINUTE AGO.

MY TEACHERS AT SCHOOL HELP ME WITH READING. THEY GIVE ME ALL KINDS OF HELP IN MANY DIFFERENT WAYS TO HELP ME READ.

SOMETIMES I'M WITH A DIFFERENT TEACHER WHO HELPS ME, SOMETIMES I AM WITH A DIFFERENT FRIEND WHO HELPS ME.

SOME OF MY FRIENDS NEED HELP WITH LEARNING TOO. THEY GET HELP WITH MATH OR WRITING PROBLEMS.

MY FRIENDS AND TEACHERS ENCOURAGE ME TO BE THE BEST READER I CAN POSSIBLY BE. I AM SO HAPPY TO HAVE THEIR HELP.

NOBODY MAKES FUN OF ME WHEN I READ, HOWEVER, I GET NERVOUS WHEN I HAVE TO.

MANY FAMOUS PEOPLE HAVE LEARNING DISABILITIES INCLUDING MOVIE STARS, PRESIDENTS, BUSINESS OWNERS AND ME!

MY NAME IS SAM. I HAVE A LEARNING DISABILITY, AND IT'S OKAY!

Printed in the United States
by Baker & Taylor Publisher Services